RØurke
Educational Media
rourkeeducationalmedia.com

A Division of
**Carson
Dellosa**
Education

ATVs

OFF-ROAD
VEHICLES

GARY SPROTT

Before Reading: *Building Background Knowledge and Vocabulary*

Building background knowledge can help children process new information and build upon what they already know. Before reading a book, it is important to tap into what children already know about the topic. This will help them develop their vocabulary and increase their reading comprehension.

Questions and Activities to Build Background Knowledge:

1. Look at the front cover of the book and read the title. What do you think this book will be about?

2. What do you already know about this topic?

3. Take a book walk and skim the pages. Look at the table of contents, photographs, captions, and bold words. Did these text features give you any information or predictions about what you will read in this book?

Vocabulary: *Vocabulary Is Key to Reading Comprehension*

Use the following directions to prompt a conversation about each word.

- Read the vocabulary words.
- What comes to mind when you see each word?
- What do you think each word means?

Vocabulary Words:
- amphibious
- chassis
- functional
- hazardous
- remote
- winch

During Reading: *Reading for Meaning and Understanding*

To achieve deep comprehension of a book, children are encouraged to use close reading strategies. During reading, it is important to have children stop and make connections. These connections result in deeper analysis and understanding of a book.

Close Reading a Text

During reading, have children stop and talk about the following:

- Any confusing parts
- Any unknown words
- Text to text, text to self, text to world connections
- The main idea in each chapter or heading

Encourage children to use context clues to determine the meaning of any unknown words. These strategies will help children learn to analyze the text more thoroughly as they read.

When you are finished reading this book, turn to the next-to-last page for **After Reading Questions** and an **Activity**.

TABLE OF CONTENTS

Tough Trailblazers...................................4

Splash Attack......................................14

Racing to the Rescue 20

Memory Game.....................................30

Index 31

After Reading Questions.....................31

Activity...31

About the Author 32

TOUGH TRAILBLAZERS

Farm paths and forest trails.
Rocky canyons and swampy valleys.
When you need a go-anywhere,
do-anything set of wheels, it's time
for an ATV (all-terrain vehicle)!

An All-Types Vehicle

ATVs can be no-frills or fancy.
These off-road vehicles come with
handlebars like a bicycle or with
a steering wheel like a car. There
are one-seaters, two-seaters,
four-seaters, and six-seaters.
There are even no-seaters!

Their ability to go off the beaten path makes all-terrain vehicles a favorite of farmers, hunters, sportspeople, soldiers, and weekend thrill-seekers. You could say an ATV puts the fun in **functional**!

functional (FUHNGK-shuh-nuhl): works well or is designed to be practical and useful

Down on the farm, ATVs are workhorses, towing and carrying equipment and supplies. The Yamaha Grizzly EPS can pull loads weighing 1,300 pounds (590 kilograms). That's almost the weight of two grizzly bears!

A Rugged Rambler

ATVs are designed to take— and survive—a pounding. With a heavy-duty **chassis** and a powerful suspension, an ATV can handle bone-jarring rides over rough surfaces.

chassis (CHAS-ee): the frame on which the body of a vehicle is built

ATVs have been around since the 1960s. The first models had three fat tires and looked like an oversized child's tricycle. Honda's All Terrain Cycle (ATC) became popular in the 1970s.

In the 1980s, the Honda ATC was nicknamed Big Red.

Reinventing the Wheel

The Suzuki QuadRunner was the first four-wheel ATV. It went on sale in 1982. The extra wheel made the vehicle more stable and more appealing to hunters and farmers.

All-wheel drive gives ATVs the traction to grip slippery surfaces. Mudding through a swamp? Scampering up a sand dune? No problem! An ATV will keep you grounded.

Packing a Punch

The Polaris RZR XP Turbo is built for extreme performance. This ATV's engine can generate 168 horsepower. That's as much power as you'd find in a family car such as a Honda Civic!

The Polaris RZR 800 goes way off the road!

SPLASH ATTACK

Sure, ATVs are built for all types of terrain. But what about water? Yup! **Amphibious** ATVs are ready to take the plunge.

---

amphibious (am-FIB-ee-uhs): able to move on land and in water

Like a Duck to Water

They had fiberglass bodies like bathtubs, six wheels, and ran on two chainsaw engines. The earliest amphibious ATVs were little duckies that could travel on land and water.

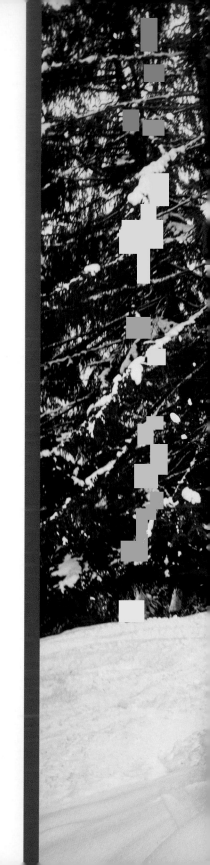

Amphibious ATVs are beasts built to tackle the toughest tasks. They can carry people into **remote** areas crossed by muddy ditches, creeks, and streams. They are used in construction, exploration, and emergency rescue. In some models, tracks can be placed over the wheels to help cross snow or mud.

---

remote (ri-MOHT): far away; secluded or isolated

The Argo Frontier 650 is a brawny eight-wheeler that can transport six people on land and four on water. It can travel 22 miles (35 kilometers) per hour over land.

Tired of Paddling?

The Frontier 650's tires have ridges like paddles. The special design helps move the ATV through water and keeps it gripping the ground in dangerous conditions.

RACING TO THE RESCUE

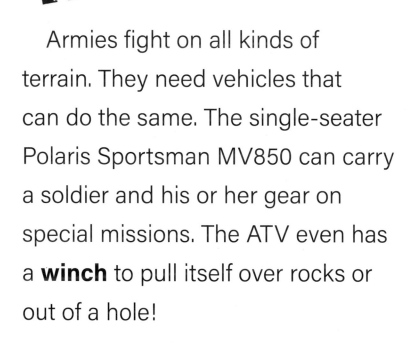

Armies fight on all kinds of terrain. They need vehicles that can do the same. The single-seater Polaris Sportsman MV850 can carry a soldier and his or her gear on special missions. The ATV even has a **winch** to pull itself over rocks or out of a hole!

winch (winch): a device that can hook, lift, and pull heavy objects; made of a cable wound around a rotating drum

The Squad Mission Support System (SMSS) is part ATV and part robot. Used for transporting military supplies, the SMSS can steer itself and follow marching soldiers without the use of remote control.

Robotic ATVs are also used in **hazardous** situations. The vehicles can be operated remotely to detect deadly gases and find explosive devices. Some can even fight fires at close range. No driver equals no danger!

hazardous (HAZ-ur-duhs): dangerous or risky

Robot to the Rescue!

Robotic ATVs can ride to the rescue in areas that are too dangerous for humans. On a snowy mountaintop, ATVs can explore holes and tunnels where people or equipment might be trapped. Onboard lasers can scan the terrain.

CAUTION
AVALANCHE AREA

RESCUE

If something has wheels and an engine, there's a good chance it's being raced somewhere. All-terrain vehicles are no exception! ATV motocross racing events attract competitors from around the world.

Roaring and Soaring!

Each year, racers kick up dirt jumping the mounds and rounding the curves in the ATV Supercross competition. The races are held at the famous Daytona International Speedway in Florida.

Riding an ATV can be thrilling—and risky. Riders must wear protective gear, including long pants, long sleeves, a helmet, gloves, boots, and goggles. They must stay off public roads and follow all laws. Many organizations offer classes for first-time riders. Rev up the fun by staying safe!

Memory Game

Look at the pictures. What do you remember reading on the pages where each image appeared?

Index

gear 20, 28

Honda 10, 12

motocross 26

Polaris 12, 20

robot(ic) 23, 24

soldier(s) 6, 20, 23

Suzuki 11

Yamaha 8

After Reading Questions

1. Name three purposes for ATVs.

2. Where is the ATV Supercross competition held?

3. In what situations are robotic ATVs useful?

4. What is special about the Argo Frontier 650's tires?

5. What features do ATVs have to help them handle rough terrain?

Activity

Draw and design a course for an all-terrain vehicle race. What obstacles or challenges are included? How long is the course? Is it an oval track or a cross-country route?

About the Author

Gary Sprott is a writer in Tampa, Florida. He has written books about ancient cultures, animals, plants, and automobiles. When he was growing up in Scotland, Gary always thought it would be cool to have a dune buggy. He still does, but he's happy with his minivan for now!

www.rourkeeducationalmedia.com

PHOTO CREDITS: Cover, page 1: ©wundervisuals; pages 4-5, 30, pages 6-7: ©irina02; pages 8-9, 30: ©Solstock; pages 10, 30: ©Degoragpn; page 11: ©StockStudioX; pages 12-13: ©pixinoo; pages 14-15: ©gmnicholas; pages 16-17: ©trek6500; pages 18-19: ©Argo; pages 20-21, 30: ©Cpl. Steven Fox; pages 22-23, 30: ©U.S. Army; pages 24-25: ©Honda North America; pages 26-27, 30: ©Frank11; pages 28-29: ©jetstream4wd

Edited by: Kim Thompson
Cover and interior design by: Rhea Magaro-Wallace

Library of Congress PCN Data

ATVs / Gary Sprott
(Off-Road Vehicles)
  ISBN 978-1-73161-454-4 (hard cover)
  ISBN 978-1-73161-255-7 (soft cover)
  ISBN 978-1-73161-559-6 (e-Book)
  ISBN 978-1-73161-664-7 (ePub)
Library of Congress Control Number: 2019932324

Rourke Educational Media
Printed in the United States of America,
North Mankato, Minnesota